The Usborne Nature Trail Book of
TREES & LEAVES

Written by Ingrid Selberg and Margaret Stephens
Consultant Editor E.H.M. Harris BSc, Dip For, FIFor,
Director of the Royal Forestry Society
Editorial revision by Margaret Stephens
Designed by Sally Burrough
Design revision by Robert Walster and Diane Thistlethwaite

Illustrated by
John Barber, Amanda Barlow, Isabel Bowring, Christine Darter,
John Francis, Victoria Gordon, Tim Hayward, Christine Howes,
Ian Jackson, Malcolm McGregor, Barbera Nicholson and
Annabel Spenceley,

Trees are everywhere. Only deserts and the tops of mountains are without them. This book tells you about trees and how to study them. It shows you the different parts of a tree, how they work and how they can help you to identify the tree.

It tells the whole story of a tree, from the moment a seed sprouts to when a mature tree dies or is cut down for timber. This book also has special tips on how to collect information and specimens.

If you want to identify a tree, look first in the sections at the back, called *Common trees you can spot*. If you fail to find a picture of your tree there, turn to the pages that deal with the part of the tree you are looking at, such as a leaf or a piece of the bark.

The Usborne Nature Trail Book of
TREES & LEAVES

Contents

How a tree grows   4
How to identify trees   6
What to look for on a tree
  Leaves   8
  Winter buds   10
  Shape   12
  Bark   13
  Flowers   14
  Fruits and seeds   16
Grow your own tree seedling   18
Forestry   19

Annual rings   20
Wood   21
Pests and fungi   22
Injuries   23
Woodland life   24
Making a tree survey   26
Common trees you can spot
  Conifers   28
  Broadleaved trees   29
Index, books and, clubs   32

First published in 1977 by:
Usborne Publishing Ltd
Usborne House
83-85 Saffron Hill
London EC1N 8RT
United Kingdom

Printed in Belgium

How a tree grows

This is the life story of a Sycamore, but all trees grow in a similar way. Although there are many different kinds of trees, they all sprout from seeds, grow larger, have flowers, form fruits and shed seeds.

You can study many of these steps in a tree's life. You can watch a tiny seedling sprout and then keep a record of its growth. You can count the girdle scars on a young tree to find out its age.

Older trees have flowers and fruits, although they may be hard to see on some trees. Not all trees have flowers as large as the Horse Chestnut's or fruits as big as the Apple tree's. Most fruits ripen in autumn, but some appear in early summer and spring.

An important part of a tree that you do not usually see is the roots. If you find an overturned tree, look at the roots and try to measure them. Look also at logs and tree stumps for the layers of wood and bark. They can tell you the age of the tree and how quickly it has grown.

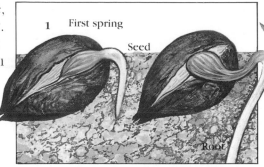

1 First spring — Seed, Root

The tree starts growing in spring from a seed which has been lying in the soil all winter. At this time, with the help of the food stored inside it, the seed sends down a root into the soil to suck up water and minerals.

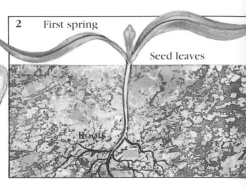

2 First spring — Seed leaves, Roots

Next, the seed sends up a tiny shoot which pokes above the ground and into the light. Two fleshy seed leaves open up with a small bud between them. These leaves are not the same shape as the tree's real leaves will be.

Buds

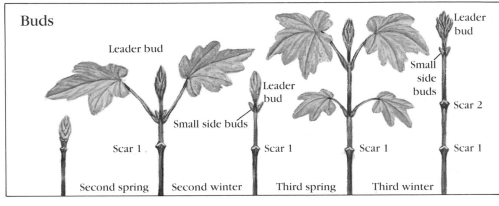

Leader bud, Small side buds, Scar 1, Second spring
Leader bud, Scar 1, Second winter
Leader bud, Scar 1, Third spring
Leader bud, Small side buds, Scar 2, Scar 1, Third winter

In the second spring, the bud opens and there are two new leaves. A new shoot grows too, with another bud at the tip. In autumn, the leaves drop off. Every year the same thing happens, and every time the leaves fall off, they leave a girdle scar on the stem. Buds on the sides of the stem also grow shoots, but they do not grow as fast as the leader shoot at the top of the tree. Each year the tree grows taller, and the roots grow deeper.

Pollen on the flowers

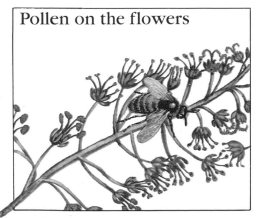

When the tree is about twelve years old, it grows flowers on its branches in the spring. Bees and other insects, searching for nectar, visit the flowers and some of the pollen from the flowers sticks on to their hairy bodies.

Fruits

When the bees visit other flowers from the same tree, some of the pollen on their bodies rubs off on to the female parts of the flowers. When the pollen and female parts are joined, the flowers are fertilized and become fruits.

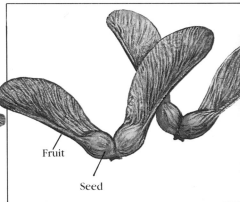

Fruit, Seed

Later that year, the fruits fall off the tree. The Sycamore fruits here spin like tiny helicopters, carrying the seeds away from the parent tree. The wings rot on the ground, and the seeds are ready to grow the following spring.

3 Leaves

Seed leaves

First summer

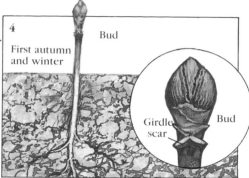

4

Bud

First autumn
and winter

Girdle
scar

Bud

The seed leaves have stored food in them to help the seedling grow. Soon the bud opens, and the first pair of real leaves appears. These will trap light from the sun to grow more food. The seed leaves then drop off. The roots grow longer.

In the autumn, all the leaves change colour and drop off, leaving a "girdle scar" around the stem where they were attached. A bud is left at the end of the shoot. The bud does not grow during the winter. It stays dormant.

Holly leaf

Many broadleaved trees are deciduous, which means that they lose their leaves in autumn. They do this because their leaves cannot work properly in cold weather, and there is not enough sunlight in winter for the leaves to make food for the tree.

Most conifers are evergreens. Their needles are tougher than most broadleaves, and they can keep making food even in the dark of winter.

A few broadleaved trees, such as Holly, are also evergreen. Like conifer needles, their leaves have a waxy coating which helps them survive the winter.

Inside a tree

Each year, a tree grows more branches. The trunk thickens by adding a new layer of wood to hold the branches up, and the roots grow deeper and wider. This picture shows you the inside of the trunk, and all its different parts.

1 Heartwood. This is old sapwood which is dead and has become very hard. It makes the tree strong and rigid.

2 Rays. In a cross-section of a log you can see pale lines. These are called rays and they carry food sideways.

3 Cambium. This layer is so thin that you can hardly see it. Its job is to make a new layer of sapwood (see page 20) each year. This makes the trunk thicker and stronger.

4 Sapwood. This layer also has tiny tubes in it which carry the sap (water and minerals) to all parts of the tree from the roots. Each year a new ring of this wood is made by the cambium.

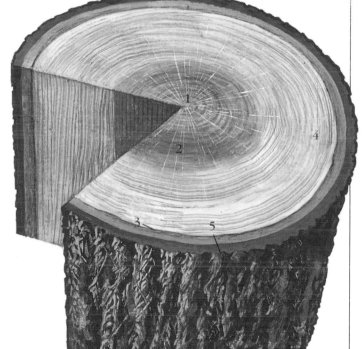

5 Phloem. Just inside the bark are tubes which carry food down from the leaves to all parts of the tree, including the roots.

6 Bark is the outer layer which protects the tree from sun, rain and fungi which might attack it.

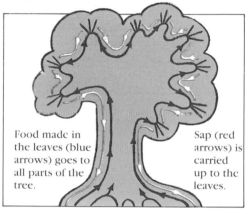

Food made in the leaves (blue arrows) goes to all parts of the tree.

Sap (red arrows) is carried up to the leaves.

To help it grow, the tree makes food for itself in the leaves, which contain a green chemical called chlorophyll. In sunlight, the chlorophyll can change oxygen from the air, water, and minerals brought up from the soil into food for the tree. If a tree gets no light to make food it will die.

Scots Pine cone

Seeds fall out of cone.

Some trees, such as the Scots Pine, have fruits called cones, which stay on the tree, but open up to let the seeds fall out by themselves. When the cones are old and dried up, they usually fall off the tree too.

How to identify trees

One of the best ways of identifying a tree is to look at its leaves. Be careful though, because some trees have leaves that are very similar. For example, a London Plane leaf could be confused with a Norway Maple leaf. So when you have named your tree just by identifying a leaf, always check that you are correct by looking at other parts of the tree, such as the flowers or bark.

Trees can be divided into three groups: broadleaved, coniferous, and palm trees (see the pictures to the right here). Try to decide which group your tree belongs to. There is something to give you clues in every season of the year. In spring and summer, look at the leaves and flowers. In autumn, look at the fruits. Winter is the best time to study buds, twigs, bark and tree shapes.

You do not need to go into a woodland or forest to study trees. Look at the many different kinds that grow in gardens, parks and roads. Sometimes you can find rare trees in gardens.

Broadleaved trees

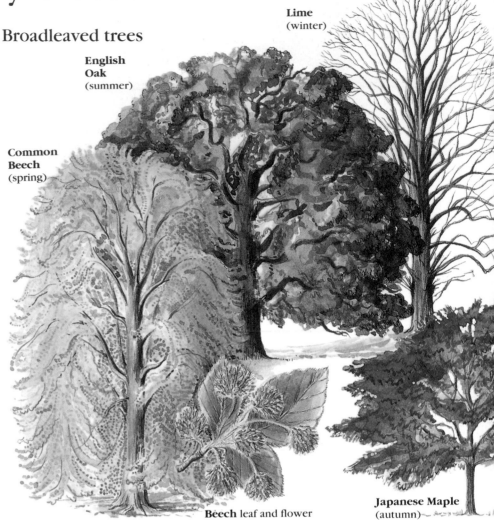

English Oak (summer)

Common Beech (spring)

Lime (winter)

Beech leaf and flower

Japanese Maple (autumn)

Most broadleaved trees have wide, flat leaves which they drop in winter. Some broadleaved trees, though, such as Holly, Laurel, Holm Oak and Box, are evergreen and keep their leaves in winter.

Broadleaved trees have seeds that are encased in fruits. The timber of broadleaved trees is called hardwood, because it is usually harder than the wood of most conifers, or softwood trees.

Tree or shrub?

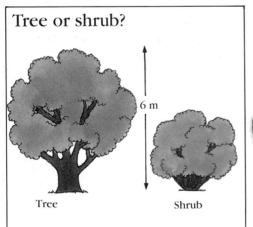

6 m

Tree

Shrub

Trees are plants that can grow to over 6 m high on a woody stem. Shrubs are generally smaller, and have several stems. See page 27 for how to measure trees.

What to look for

Leaves

Yew (conifer)

Common Beech (broadleaf)

Oak (broadleaf)

The leaves will give you the biggest clue to the identity of the tree, but look at other parts of the tree as well. There is a guide to leaves on page 8.

Shape and bark

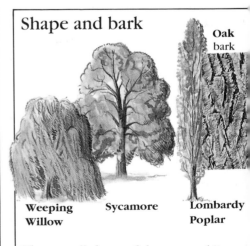

Oak bark

Weeping Willow

Sycamore

Lombardy Poplar

The overall shape of the tree and its crown is also a good clue (see page 12) Some trees can be identified just by looking at their bark.

Conifers

Scots Pine

Cone and needles

Norway Spruce

European Larch (in winter)

European Larch (in summer)

Palms

Leaf

Canary Palm

Most conifers have narrow, needle-like or scaly leaves, and are evergreen, that is they keep their leaves in winter. The larch is one conifer that is not evergreen, as the tree loses its leaves in winter.

Conifer fruits are usually woody cones, but some conifers, such as the Yew, have berry-like fruits. The overall shape of conifers is more regular and symmetrical than the shape of most broadleaved trees.

Palms have trunks that have no branches. They look like giant stalks. The leaves grow from the top of the tree. Unlike other trees, palms grows taller without getting thicker.

Winter buds

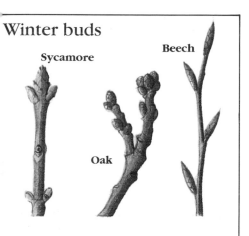

Sycamore

Beech

Oak

In winter, when there are often no leaves to look at, you can identify some trees from their buds, bark and shape. See page 11 for bud shapes.

Flowers

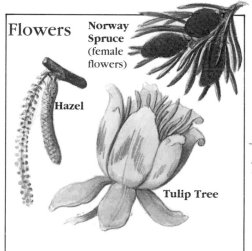

Norway Spruce (female flowers)

Hazel

Tulip Tree

In certain seasons a tree's flowers can help you to identify it. But some trees do not flower every year. For tree flowers, see pages 14-15.

Fruits and seeds

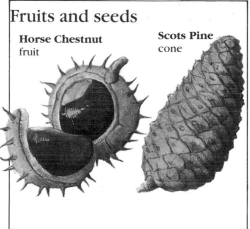

Horse Chestnut fruit

Scots Pine cone

All trees have fruits bearing seeds which may grow into new trees. This Horse Chestnut conker and the pine cone are both fruits. See pages 16-17.

Leaves

One of the things that most people notice about a tree is its leaves. A big Oak tree has more than 250,000 leaves and a conifer tree may have many millions of needles.

The leaves fan out to catch as much sunlight as possible. With the green chlorophyll inside them, they make food for the tree. They take in gases from the air through tiny holes, and give out water vapour and gases in the same way. Once the food is made, it is carried through veins to other parts of the leaf. The veins make the leaf strong like a skeleton.

The leaf stem carries water from the twig and also helps the leaf to move into the light. It is tough so that the leaf does not break off in strong winds.

The leaves of broadleaved trees and conifers look different, but they do the same work. Most conifer leaves can survive the winter, but the leaves of most broadleaves fall off in the autumn. A conifer needle stays on a tree for about three to five years.

Tracking down your mystery leaf

1. Decide if the leaf is from a conifer or a broadleaved tree.

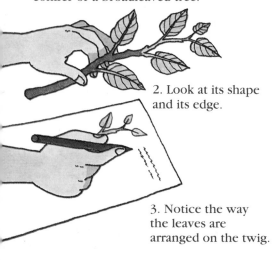

2. Look at its shape and its edge.

3. Notice the way the leaves are arranged on the twig.

4. Look at the colour and leaf surface.

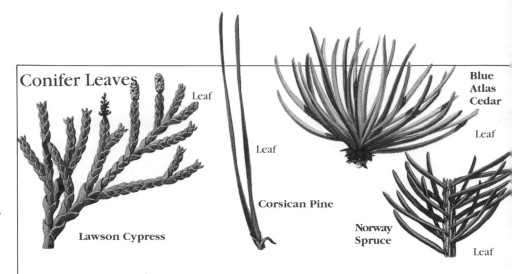

Conifer Leaves

Lawson Cypress

Corsican Pine

Norway Spruce

Blue Atlas Cedar

Leaf

Here you can see three types of conifer leaf. Many conifers have narrow needle-like leaves which are either single, in small bunches or in clusters. They can be very sharp and spiky. But other conifers, such as the Cypresses, have tiny scale-like leaves, overlaping one another.

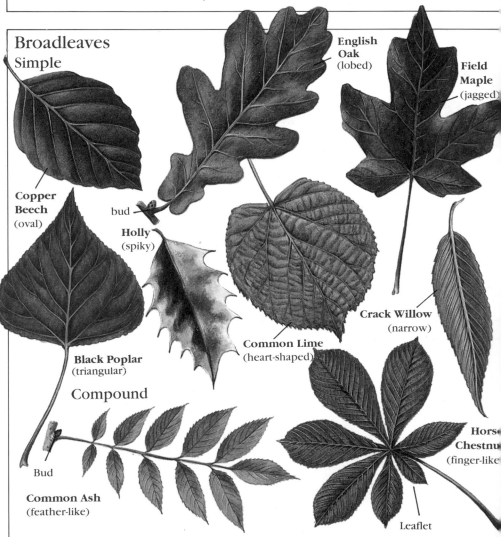

Broadleaves
Simple

Copper Beech (oval)

bud

Holly (spiky)

English Oak (lobed)

Field Maple (jagged)

Common Lime (heart-shaped)

Crack Willow (narrow)

Black Poplar (triangular)

Compound

Bud

Common Ash (feather-like)

Horse Chestnut (finger-like)

Leaflet

The leaves of broadleaved trees have many different shapes. Leaves in one piece are called simple. Those made up of many leaflets, such as Common Ash and Horse Chestnut shown here, are called compound. Simple leaves and compound leaves both have one bud at the base of their stems.

These leaves are not drawn to the same scale

8

Opposite

Dawn
Redwood

Alternate

Silver
Birch

Horse
Chestnut

Copper
beach

Maidenhair Tree

Rowan

Red Oak

Common Pear

Underside

White Poplar

Magnified veins
of underside

Twigs

Leaves are arranged on twigs in various
ways. They can be opposite each other in
pairs, or they can be single and alternate
from one side of the twig to the other.

Colour

Leaves are green because of the
chlorophyll inside them. In autumn, the
chlorophyll in broadleaves decays. They
change colour before they fall.

Leaf close-up

Leaves have a network of tiny veins. Their
upper surface is tough and often glossy, to
stop the sun from drying them out. The
underside is often hairy.

Leaf scrapbook

Heavy object

Blotting paper

Leaf skeleton

Keep a scrapbook of the leaves you
find. Place each leaf between two
sheets of blotting paper. Then put a
book and a heavy object on top.

Leave them for about a week. When
the leaves are flat and dry, mount them
in a scrapbook with sticky tape. Label
the leaves and write down where and

when you found them. When a dead
leaf has crumbled, the strong stem and
veins remain as a skeleton. You will
often find these in winter.

Leaf tiles

Press the leaf on to
the "clay" with a
rolling pin.

The finished tile can be
painted or varnished.

Make your clay by mixing together:
2 cups flour (not self-raising)
1 cup salt
1 cup water
2 tablespoons cooking oil

Scatter some flour onto a surface top
and shape your "clay" into a ball. Roll it
out flat with a floured rolling pin, until
it is about 2 cm thick. Press your leaf,
vein side down, onto the clay so that it

leaves a mark. Remove the leaf and
bake the clay in the oven at 150°C
(250°F) for about two hours. When the
tile has cooled, you can paint it or
varnish it.

Winter buds

Most broadleaved trees have no leaves in winter, but you can still identify them by their winter buds. These contain the beginnings of a shoot, leaves and flowers, which will appear in the next year.

The thick, overlapping bud scales protect a shoot from the cold and from attack by insects. In places where winter is the dry season, the bud scales keep a new shoot from drying out. If the tiny undeveloped leaf has no bud scales, it may be covered with furry hairs to protect it.

In spring, when it gets warmer, a new shoot swells and breaks open the protective hard scales. At the end of the growing season, each shoot will have a new winter bud at the tip. There are many buds on a twig. The leading bud, which is usually at the tip, contains the shoot which will grow most. Shoots become twigs and eventually branches.

Other buds hold leaves and flowers. They are also reserves in case the leading bud is damaged.

Inside a bud there are tiny leaves and flowers, all folded up. If you cut a bud in half and look at it through a lens, you can see the different parts.

Outer scales of bud.

Leaf

Complete flower head.

This is a three-year-old Horse Chestnut twig. You can tell its age by counting the girdle scars. It has large brown buds in opposite pairs. The bud scales are sticky.

This side bud will not grow into a twig unless the leading bud is damaged.

The leading bud contains next year's shoot.

A leaf scar left by last year's leaf.

This side twig is two years old.

Last year's leading bud was here. Notice the girdle scar.

Leading bud

These buds will become leaves.

One year's growth.

Last year's buds were here.

An undeveloped twig.

A two-year-old **Norway Spruce** tw

Forcing buds indoors

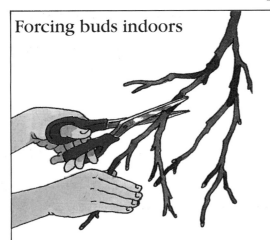

You can "force" buds to open in winter or early spring by bringing them indoors. The best ones to try are Horse Chestnut, Birch, Willow and Forsythia.

Cut the twigs with scissors. Don't break them! Always ask the owner before cutting and don't take too much. Place twigs in water in a vase or jam jar. Place

them in a sunny spot indoors, then wait for the buds to open. This may take some weeks. Draw the buds before and after they have opened.

Winter bud indentification chart

What to look for

If you try to identify trees by their winter buds, you will see that they vary a great deal. Here is a list of things to look for:

1. How are the buds positioned on the twig? Like leaves, buds can be in opposite pairs or single and alternate.

2. What colour are the buds and the twig?

3. What shape is the twig? Are the buds pointed or rounded?

4. Is the bud covered with hairs or scales? If there are scales, how many? Is the bud sticky?

Ash. Smooth, grey twig. Large, black opposite buds.

Sycamore. Large, green, opposite buds with dark-edged scales.

Beech. Slender twig. Alternate, spiky, brown buds sticking out.

False Acacia. Grey twig. Thorns next to tiny, alternate buds.

Willow. Slender twig. Alternate buds close to twig.

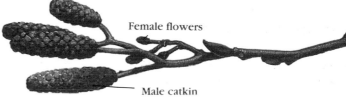

Female flowers

Male catkin

Common Alder. Alternate, stalked, purple buds often with male catkins.

English Elm. Zigzag twig. Alternate, blackish-red buds.

White Poplar. Twig and alternate buds covered with white down.

Common Lime. Zigzag twig. Alternate, reddish buds with two scales.

Walnut. Thick, hollow twig. Big, black, velvety, alternate buds.

Sweet Chestnut. Knobbly twig. Large, reddish, alternate buds.

Turkey Oak. Clusters of alternate buds with whiskers.

London Plane. Alternate, cone-shaped buds. Ring scar around bud.

Wild Cherry. Large, glossy, red buds grouped at tip of twig.

Magnolia. Huge, furry, green-grey buds.

These twigs are drawn life size.

Whitebeam. Downy, green, alternate buds.

Shape

Look at all these different tree shapes. Each type of tree has its own typical shape made up from the arrangement and shape of its branches. Winter is the best time of year to see the shapes of broadleaved trees because their branches are not hidden by leaves.

Practise making quick shape sketches when you are outside.

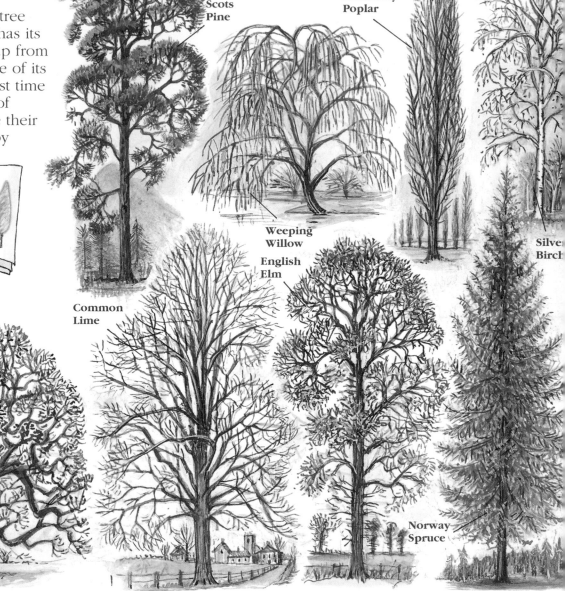

Scots Pine

Weeping Willow

Lombardy Poplar

Silver Birch

Common Lime

English Elm

Norway Spruce

English Oak

How trees are shaped

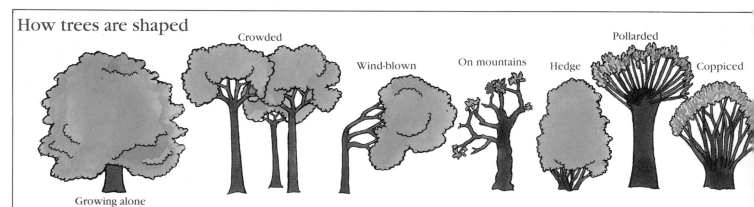

Growing alone

Crowded

Wind-blown

On mountains

Hedge

Pollarded

Coppiced

Trees grow a wide crown or top, so their leaves will get lots of sunlight. Where trees crowd together, they grow thin and tall to try and reach the light. Weather changes the shape of trees. Steady wind from one direction or salty sea winds can make trees grow bent and one-sided. On mountains, trees are dwarfed and gnarled by the cold and drying wind. Trees are also pruned or cut by man to grow in special ways. Pollarding means cutting off the branches of a tree. Coppicing is cutting the trunk down to the ground. This causes long, new shoots to grow.

Bark

The outside of the tree is covered in a hard, tough layer of bark. It protects the tree from drying out and from damage by insects or animals. It also keeps the inside of the tree at a steady temperature. Under the bark there are tubes (phloem) carrying food (sap) which can be damaged if the bark is stripped off. If this happens, the tree may die.

When the tree is young, the bark is thin and smooth, but with age it thickens and forms different patterns. You can identify trees by their bark.

How bark patterns form

The old bark splits and new bark forms underneath.

Bark is dead and cannot grow or stretch. As wood inside the bark grows outwards, the bark splits, peels or cracks in a way that is special to each type of tree.

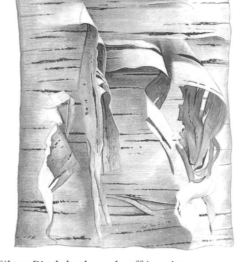

Silver Birch bark peels off in wispy strips that look like ribbons.

English Oak bark has deep ridges and cracks.

The bark of Scots Pine flakes off in large pieces.

Beech has smooth thin bark, which flakes off in tiny pieces.

Bark rubbings

Sticky tape

You need strong thin paper, sticky tape and wax crayons or heel-ball. Tape the paper securely to the tree. Rub firmly with the crayon, but do not tear the paper. Watch the bark pattern appear.

Candle

Rubbing that has been painted.

You can also rub the paper with candle wax. Then at home, paint over the rubbing done in this way. The bark pattern will stay the colour of the candle.

Cork

The bark of the Cork Oak is so thick that it can be removed without damaging the tree. Cork is used in many ways to keep in moisture and to resist heat. Table mats are often made from cork.

Flowers

All trees produce flowers in order to make seeds that can grow into new trees. The flowers vary from tree to tree in size, shape and colour. Some are so small that you may not notice them.

Flowers have male parts called stamens and female parts called ovaries. The stamen produces pollen, while the ovary contains ovules. When pollen from the stamen reaches the ovules in the ovary, the flower is fertilized. Fertilized flowers grow into fruits which contain seeds.

Flowers which have both ovaries and stamens, such as the Cherry, are called "perfect". On other trees the ovaries and the stamens are in different flowers. Then, the female flowers grow in separate clusters to male the flowers. The clusters can be cone shaped or long and dangling. A few trees, such as Yew, Holly and Willow, have their male and female flowers on entirely separate trees.

Parts of a flower

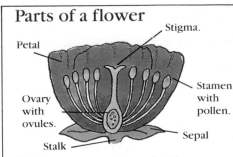

This is a cross-section of a Cherry blossom, which is a typical "perfect" flower as it has male and female parts.

European Larch

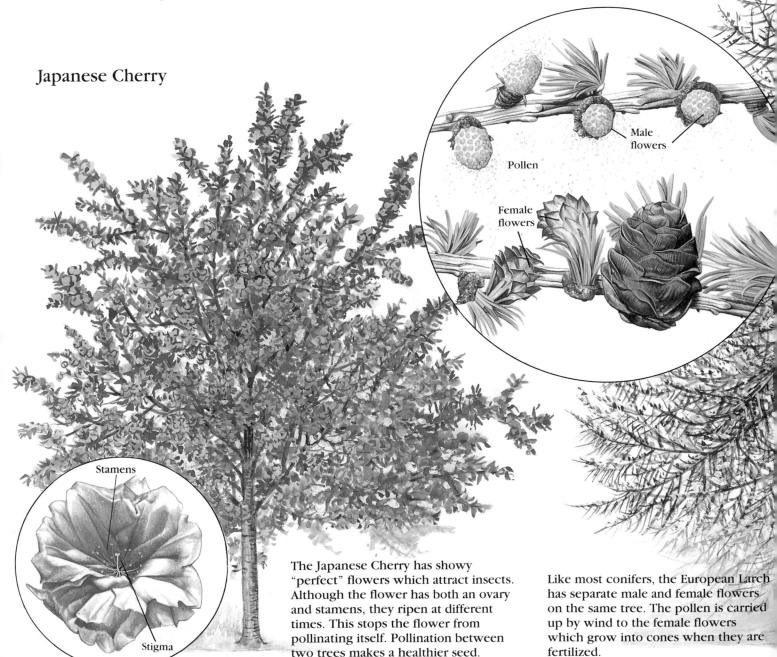

Japanese Cherry

The Japanese Cherry has showy "perfect" flowers which attract insects. Although the flower has both an ovary and stamens, they ripen at different times. This stops the flower from pollinating itself. Pollination between two trees makes a healthier seed.

Like most conifers, the European Larch has separate male and female flowers on the same tree. The pollen is carried up by wind to the female flowers which grow into cones when they are fertilized.

14

Pollination

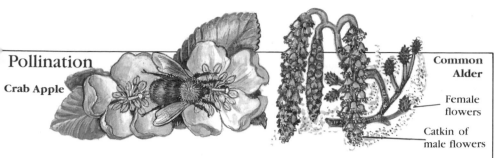

Crab Apple

Common Alder

Female flowers

Catkin of male flowers

Some flowers are pollinated by insects. Insects, feeding on flowers, accidentally pick up pollen on their bodies. The pollen rubs off on the next flower they visit. This is called cross-pollination. Most catkins and conifer flowers are wind-pollinated. They are small and dull because they do not need to attract insects. The wind blows pollen off the long stamens, and the sticky stigmas at the end of each ovary catch the pollen.

Fertilization

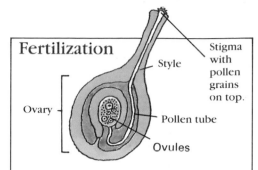

Stigma with pollen grains on top.

Style

Ovary

Pollen tube

Ovules

Once the pollen grains have reached the stigma, they make tubes down to the ovary. There they fertilize the ovules, which later become seeds.

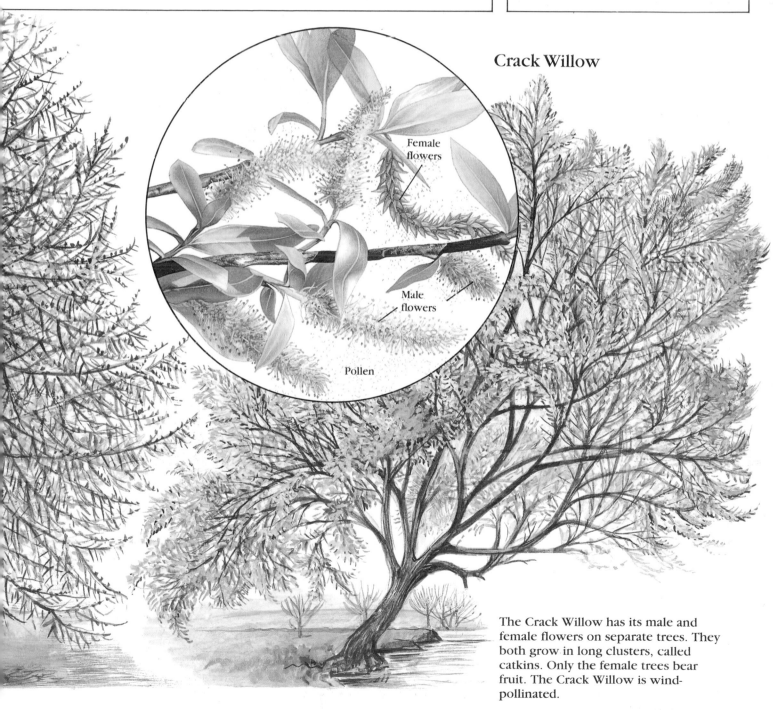

Crack Willow

Female flowers

Male flowers

Pollen

The Crack Willow has its male and female flowers on separate trees. They both grow in long clusters, called catkins. Only the female trees bear fruit. The Crack Willow is wind-pollinated.

Fruits and seeds

Fruits containing seeds grow from fertilized flowers. An apple and the prickly conker case of the Horse Chestnut are both fruits. They look different, but they do the same job, protecting the seeds and helping them to spread to a place where they can grow.

Broadleaved trees have fruits which completely encase their seeds. These fruits can come in many different forms, such as nuts, berries and soft fruits. Conifer seeds are uncovered and not in a fruit that encases them. They are usually held in a scaly cone.

Many fruits and cones are damaged by insects and disease, eaten by birds and animals, or fall off the trees before they can ripen. The seeds inside undamaged healthy fruits ripen in the autumn. They need to get far away from the parent tree, as it will take all the food and light.

Seeds are spread by birds, animals, wind and water. Very few seeds ever get to a place where they can reach full growth. About one in a million acorns becomes an Oak tree.

How a cone ripens

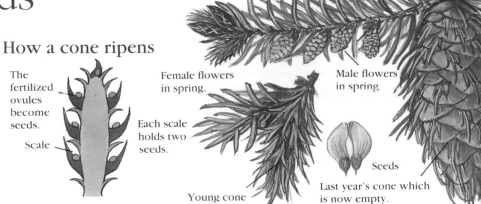

The fertilized ovules become seeds.

Scale

Cross-section of a cone.

Female flowers in spring.

Each scale holds two seeds.

Young cone in summer.

Male flowers in spring.

Seeds

Last year's cone which is now empty.

Douglas Fir

Cones develop from the female flowers. After pollination, the scales harden and close. The stalk often bends, so the cone hangs down. The cone turns from green to brown. When the seeds are ripe and the weather is warm and dry, the scales open. The seeds flutter out on papery wings. Most cones stay on the tree for a year. Others take two years to ripen, and some remain after the seeds have gone.

Fruits of conifers

Most cones have woody scales and vary in size from 1 cm to 35 cm, and can weigh as much as 2 kg. See how many different kinds of cones you can collect.

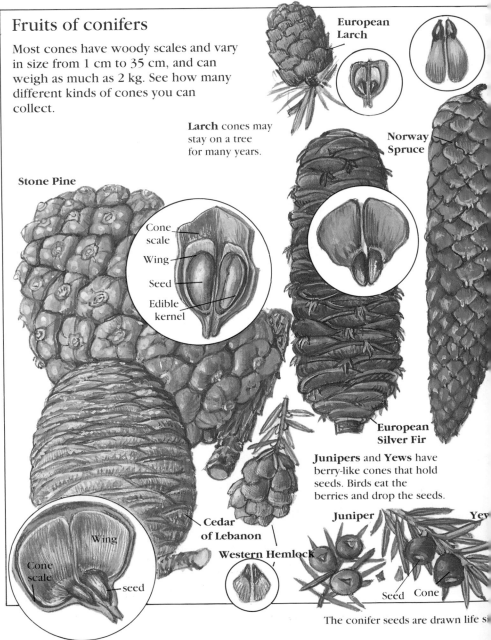

European Larch

Larch cones may stay on a tree for many years.

Norway Spruce

Stone Pine

Cone scale
Wing
Seed
Edible kernel

European Silver Fir

Junipers and **Yews** have berry-like cones that hold seeds. Birds eat the berries and drop the seeds.

Wing
Cone scale
seed

Cedar of Lebanon

Western Hemlock

Juniper

Yew

Seed   Cone

The conifer seeds are drawn life si[ze]

Scots Pine

Cones open in warm, dry weather to release the seeds. If it is wet, the scales close. Find a cone and make it open by placing it near a heater. Then put it in a damp place, and it will close.

How the fruit of a Peach tree ripens

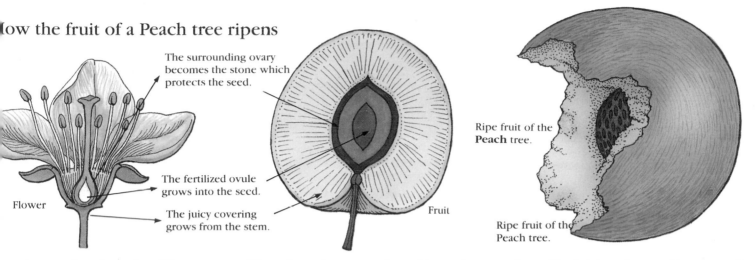

The surrounding ovary becomes the stone which protects the seed.

The fertilized ovule grows into the seed.

The juicy covering grows from the stem.

Flower

Fruit

Ripe fruit of the **Peach** tree.

Ripe fruit of the Peach tree.

The pictures show how the different parts of a flower grow into the different parts of fruit. The flower is from a Peach tree.

Water from the stem and sunshine make the fleshy part of the fruit swell. As the fruit ripens, it turns golden pink and

softens. The bright colour and sweet smell attract animals or people, who eat the juicy outer layer and throw away the stone.

Fruits of broadleaved trees

Broadleaved trees produce many different kinds of fruits. Some are nuts with hard outer shells, some are soft fruits, some are pods, some have wings or hairs.

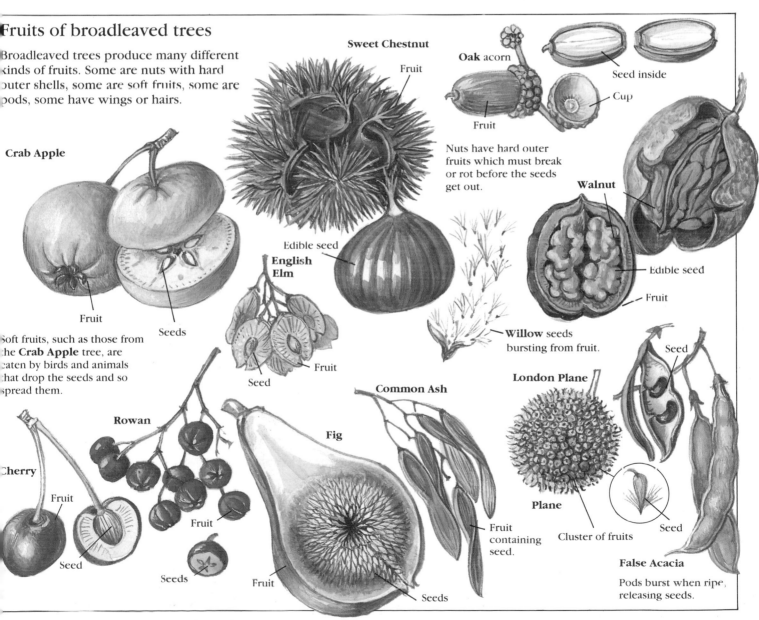

Sweet Chestnut

Fruit

Oak acorn

Fruit

Seed inside

Cup

Nuts have hard outer fruits which must break or rot before the seeds get out.

Walnut

Edible seed

Edible seed

Fruit

Crab Apple

Fruit

Seeds

Soft fruits, such as those from the **Crab Apple** tree, are eaten by birds and animals that drop the seeds and so spread them.

Edible seed

English Elm

Fruit

Seed

Willow seeds bursting from fruit.

London Plane

Seed

Rowan

Cherry

Fruit

Seed

Fruit

Seeds

Fig

Fruit

Seeds

Common Ash

Fruit containing seed.

Plane

Cluster of fruits

Seed

False Acacia

Pods burst when ripe, releasing seeds.

The cones and fruits are drawn two thirds life size.

Grow your own tree seedling

Try growing your own tree from a seed. Pick ripe seeds from trees or collect them from the ground if you know that they are fresh. The time a seed takes to sprout varies, but an acorn takes about two months. Some seeds, like those from conifers, may need to lie in the ground for over a year. Once the seedling has sprouted, keep a diary of its growth with drawings or photographs.

What you need

Flowerpots

Stones

Plastic bags

String or rubber band.

Soil

What to plant

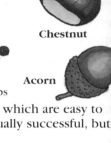

Sycamore

Chestnut

Acorn

Apple and Orange pips

Here are some seeds which are easy to grow. Acorns are usually successful, but try anything!

1 Soak acorns or other hard nuts in warm water overnight. Peel off the hard outer shells. Do not cut shells from nuts.

2 Put a handful of stones in the bottom of your pot. This is to help the water to drain properly. Place a saucer under the pot.

3 Fill a pot with some soil, or compost, until it is about two thirds full. Water the soil until it is moist, but not soggy.

4 Place one acorn, or other nut, on top of the soil. They need lots of room to grow, so only put one acorn in each pot.

5 Cover the acorn, or other nut, with a layer of soil. This layer should be about as thick as the acorn itself.

Fasten with string or rubber band

6 Place a plastic bag over the pot. This will keep the seed moist without watering. Put the pot in a sunny place and wait.

The soil should be moist, but not wet.

7 As soon as the seedling appears, remove the plastic bag. Water the seedling once or twice a week.

8 In the summer, put your seedling outside, if you can. In autumn, plant it in the ground. (You can leave it in its pot.)

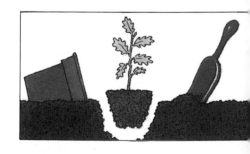

9 Dig a hole a bit larger than the pot. Gently lift out the seedling and soil from the pot. Plant it in the hole and water it.

Forestry

Trees have been growing on Earth for about 350 million years. Much land was once covered by natural forests, but they have been cut down for timber and cleared. New forests are often planted to replace the trees that have been cut down.

Because conifers grow faster than broadleaved trees and produce straight timber, they are preferred for wood production.

On this page you can read about the story of a Douglas Fir plantation, and what the foresters do to care for the trees.

Seedbeds

The seeds are sown in seedbeds. When the seedlings are 15-20 cm high, they are planted in rows in another bed where they have more room. They are weeded regularly.

Planting out

When the seedlings are about 50 cm high, they are planted out in the forest ground, which has been cleared and ploughed. There are about 2,500 trees per hectare.

Fire towers on hills help to spot fire - the forest's worst enemy. Fires can be started by a carelessly dropped match or an unguarded campfire.

Plantations can be sprayed with weedkillers and fertilizers from the air.

When the trees are felled, they are taken away to sawmills to be cut up.

Every few years the weaker trees are weeded out to give more light and room to the stronger ones. These thinnings are used for poles or are made into paper.

Trees are felled when they are fully grown (about 70 years for conifers and 150 years for Oaks). About one in every ten trees reaches its full growth.

Dead and lower branches are cut off trees. This lessens the risk of fire and stops knots from forming in the wood.

Annual rings

Inside the bark is the wood which is made up of many layers (see page 5). Each year the cambium makes a ring of wood on its inner side and grows outwards. This layer is called an annual ring. The early wood made in spring is pale and has wide tubes (phloem) to carry sap. Late wood, which is formed in summer, is darker and stronger. In wet years, the layers of wood are broad and the annual rings are far apart, but in dry years they are narrow. They are also narrow if the trees are not thinned.

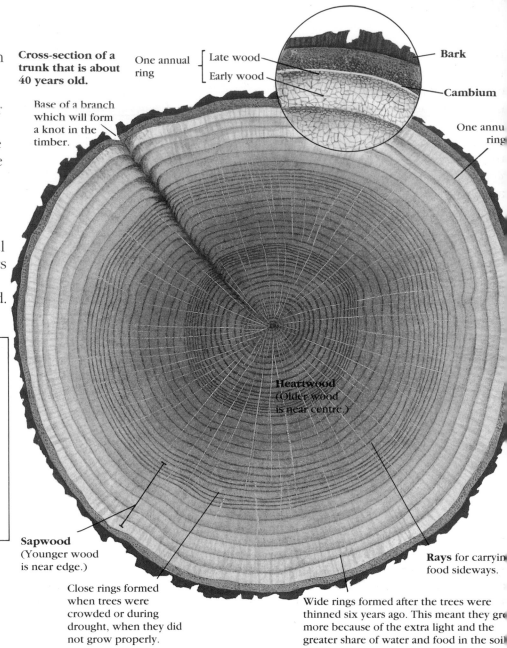

Cross-section of a trunk that is about 40 years old.

One annual ring { Late wood / Early wood

Base of a branch which will form a knot in the timber.

Bark

Cambium

One annual ring

Heartwood (Older wood is near centre.)

Sapwood (Younger wood is near edge.)

Close rings formed when trees were crowded or during drought, when they did not grow properly.

Rays for carrying food sideways.

Wide rings formed after the trees were thinned six years ago. This meant they grew more because of the extra light and the greater share of water and food in the soil.

Palms

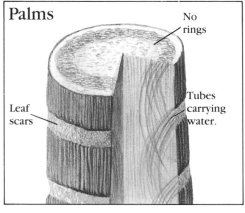

No rings

Leaf scars

Tubes carrying water.

Palm trees do not have annual rings because they have no cambium to grow new wood. Their trunks are like giant stalks which do not grow thicker.

How old is a tree?

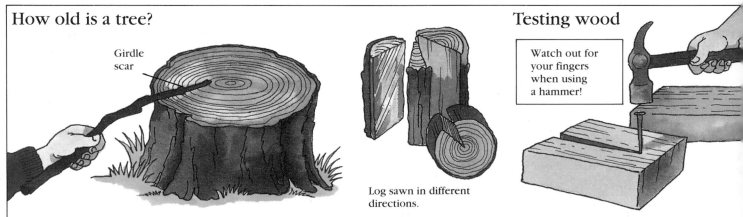

Girdle scar

Log sawn in different directions.

Testing wood

Watch out for your fingers when using a hammer!

You can find out the age of a tree by counting the annual rings in a cross-section of its trunk, as in this tree stump here. It is easiest to count the dark rings

of late wood. Twigs also have annual layers. Cut off a twig on the slant and count its rings. Then count the girdle scars on the outside. Do they agree?

Saw a small log in different ways and look at the patterns the wood makes. Test the strength of different woods by hammering nails into them.

Wood

The wood inside different types of trees varies in colour and pattern, just as the bark varies. Different kinds of wood are suited for certain uses. Wood from conifers, called softwood, is mainly used for building and making paper. Wood from broadleaved trees, called hardwood, is used to make furniture.

At the sawmill, the person operating the saw decides the best way to cut each log. A log can be made into many different sizes of planks, as well as into paper pulp.

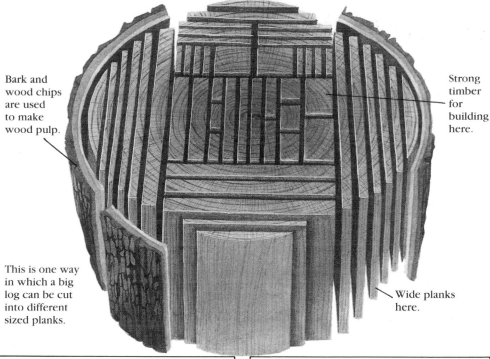

Bark and wood chips are used to make wood pulp.

Strong timber for building here.

This is one way in which a big log can be cut into different sized planks.

Wide planks here.

Grain

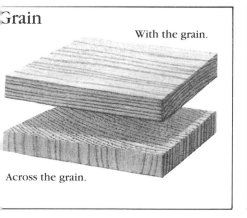

With the grain.

Across the grain.

When a plank is cut from a log, the annual rings make vertical lines which may be wavy or straight. This pattern is called the grain. Wood cut with the grain is stronger than wood cut across the grain..

Knots

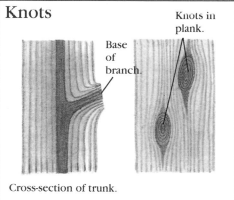

Knots in plank.

Base of branch.

Cross-section of trunk.

In a plank you may notice dark spots, called knots. This is where the base of a branch was buried in the trunk of the tree. This distorts and colours the grain, and so leaves a knot.

Seasoning

Air gets in between the timber.

Fresh wood contains water which is why green logs spit in the fire. As wood dries, it shrinks and often cracks or warps. Planks must be dried out, or seasoned, before they can be used.

Processed wood

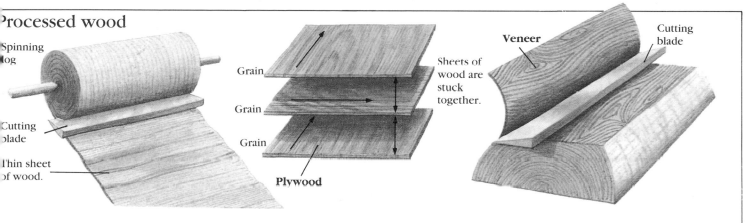

Spinning log

Cutting blade

Thin sheet of wood.

Grain

Grain

Grain

Plywood

Sheets of wood are stuck together.

Veneer

Cutting blade

Much of the wood that you see around you has been "processed". Plywood is thin layers of wood which are glued together with the grain lying in different directions. It is stronger than ordinary wood and does not warp. The thin sheet of wood is peeled off the log like a Swiss roll. Veneer is a thin sheet of wood with a beautiful grain which is used on the surface of plain furniture. Chipboard (not shown) is made of small chips and shavings mixed with glue.

Pests and fungi

Trees are attacked by insects and diseases caused by fungi. Insects use trees for food and shelter, and as places to breed. They can cause serious damage to trees, but they rarely kill them.

Fungi are a group of plants which do not flower. Mushrooms are fungi. Because fungi cannot make their own food, they may feed off plants and animals, and sometimes kill them. Fungi spread by releasing microscopic spores, like seeds, into the tree. These spores can spread and rot the tree.

Leaves and shoots

Spangle galls

Cherry g

Pine Looper

Gall Wasp

Green Tortrix

Kidney galls

Pine Sawfly

The **Tent Caterpillar** lives in a "tent", which it spins among the branches.

Oak apple galls

Some insects lay their eggs in leaves or shoots. The tree forms swellings, called galls, around the eggs. The larvae feed inside the galls

Larva

Nut Weevils lay their eggs inside nuts, where the larvae grow.

Many moth and butterfly caterpillars and other larvae eat leaves. Often each species only feeds on a certain type of tree.

Leaf Roller

Leaf Miner

Adult Nut Weevil

Aphid

Leaf Miners eat tunnels through leaves. **Leaf Rollers** fold leaves over themselves for protection.

"Pineapple" gall

An **Aphid** made this "pineapple" gall by piercing a shoot to suck out the sap.

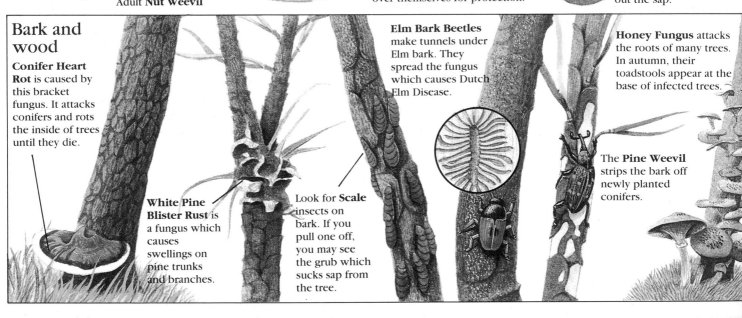

Bark and wood

Conifer Heart Rot is caused by this bracket fungus. It attacks conifers and rots the inside of trees until they die.

White Pine Blister Rust is a fungus which causes swellings on pine trunks and branches.

Look for **Scale** insects on bark. If you pull one off, you may see the grub which sucks sap from the tree.

Elm Bark Beetles make tunnels under Elm bark. They spread the fungus which causes Dutch Elm Disease.

Honey Fungus attacks the roots of many trees. In autumn, their toadstools appear at the base of infected trees.

The **Pine Weevil** strips the bark off newly planted conifers.

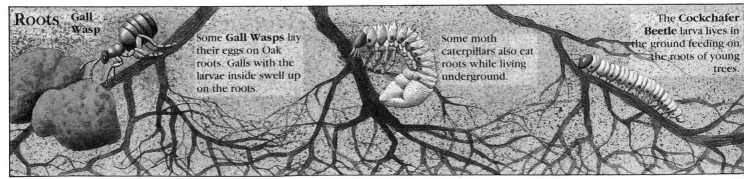

Roots

Gall Wasp

Some **Gall Wasps** lay their eggs on Oak roots. Galls with the larvae inside swell up on the roots.

Some moth caterpillars also eat roots while living underground.

The **Cockchafer Beetle** larva lives in the ground feeding on the roots of young trees.

Keeping an Oak apple gall

Netting top tied on with string.

Release **Wasp** when it emerges.

Oak Apple

In summer, collect Oak apples and other galls which do not have holes in them. Keep them in a jar with netting on top. The wasps living inside the galls should emerge in a month.

Making spore prints

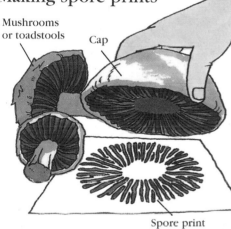

Mushrooms or toadstools

Cap

Spore print

Try using coloured paper too.

Make spore prints from mushrooms. Cut off the stalk and place the cap on some paper. Leave it overnight. It will release its spores on the paper, leaving a print. Always wash your hands after handling a fungus.

Injuries

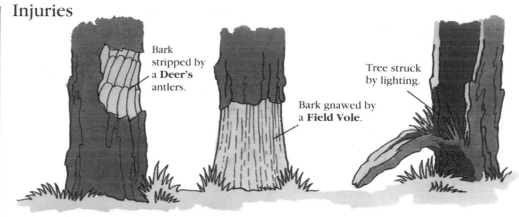

Bark stripped by a **Deer's** antlers.

Bark gnawed by a **Field Vole**.

Tree struck by lighting.

Sometimes trees are damaged by animals. Deer strip the bark off trees when they scrape the "velvet" off their antlers. Squirrels, voles and rabbits eat young bark, which can kill young saplings. If lightning strikes a tree, the trunk often cracks. This happens because the sap gets so hot that it becomes steam. It expands and then explodes, shattering the tree.

How a tree heals itself

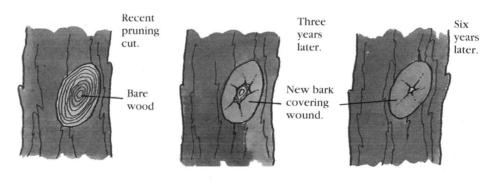

Recent pruning cut.

Bare wood

Three years later.

New bark covering wound.

Six years later.

If a branch is pruned off a tree properly, the wound usually heals. A new rim of bark grows from the cambium around the cut. This finished seal will keep out fungi and diseases. It takes years for a wound to heal. But if a wound completely surrounds the trunk, the tree will die because its food supply is cut off. This can happen when animals strip off the bark.

How trees die

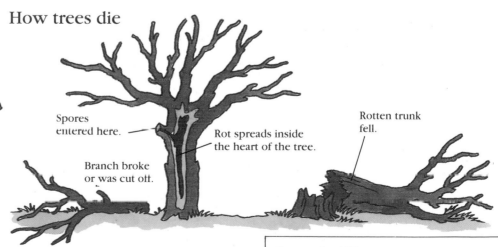

Spores entered here.

Rot spreads inside the heart of the tree.

Rotten trunk fell.

Branch broke or was cut off.

Fungus kills many trees. Spores in the air enter an opening and spread through the tree. The heartwood rots until the tree dies and falls down.

Remember! Never carve your initials or anything else on a tree. It looks ugly and can leave an opening for fungi to enter.

Woodland life

The forest is home to many plants and animals. Trees protect wildlife from bad weather, wind and too much sun. Fallen leaves and twigs make a rich soil called humus. This helps plants to grow. The wildlife in broadleaved and coniferous forests is not the same, although it may overlap.

Trees change carbon dioxide into oxygen. Chopping down trees leaves too much carbon dioxide in the atmosphere which is bad for our planet, making it warmer. This is called the "greenhouse" effect.

A coniferous forest

A coniferous forest is dark and dense. Few plants grow on the ground because of the thick layer of needles and the lack of light. Here are some animals and plants you might see in a coniferous forest.

Pine Marten

Squirrel's drey

Long-eared Owl's nest

Long-eared Ow

Great Spotted Woodpecker

Red Deer

Crossbill

Bracken

Black Grouse

Fox

Norway spruce cones

Wood Ant-hill

Broad Buckler Fern

Timberman

Goldcrest

Fly Agaric

Treecreeper

Lichen

Red Squirrel

Black Slug

A broadleaved forest

A broadleaved forest is more light and open and so attracts many more plants and animals. There are many flowers in spring before the trees' leaves have blocked out the light. As you can see, an Oak wood supports many different kinds of wildlife.

Tree roots help to hold the soil firm. If forests are cut down and the land cleared, the soil can become very loose and dry. This is called erosion.

Mistletoe

Nuthatch

Green Woodpecker

Rook in nest

Tawny Owl

Blue Tit

Long-eared Bat in tree

Poor Man's Beefsteak

Oak

Wood Anemone

Roe Deer

Badger

Bluebells

Rabbit

Pheasant

Ivy

Common Shrew

Hedgehog

Primrose

oss

Common Toad

Earthworm

Greater Stag Beetle

Speckled Wood Butterfly

Making a tree survey

You will gather many interesting facts about trees and the wildlife they shelter by doing a tree survey. Start with a small area and choose one that has many trees of different types. A piece of countryside, a park, garden or street will all do.

With a friend, make a rough map of your area and add any landmarks, such as roads or buildings. Try to work out a scale for your map - 2 cm for every 50 paces is a good one. Plot each tree on your map and be careful not to miss any.

What to take

Notebook

Tree field guide

Tape measure

Pencils

String

Identifying a tree

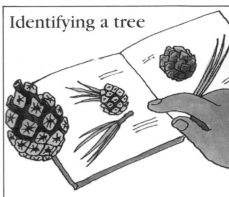

Try to identify the trees using this book or another guide (see page 32). Remember that there are many clues to help you identify them. One type of clue, such as a leaf, is not enough.

Making a map

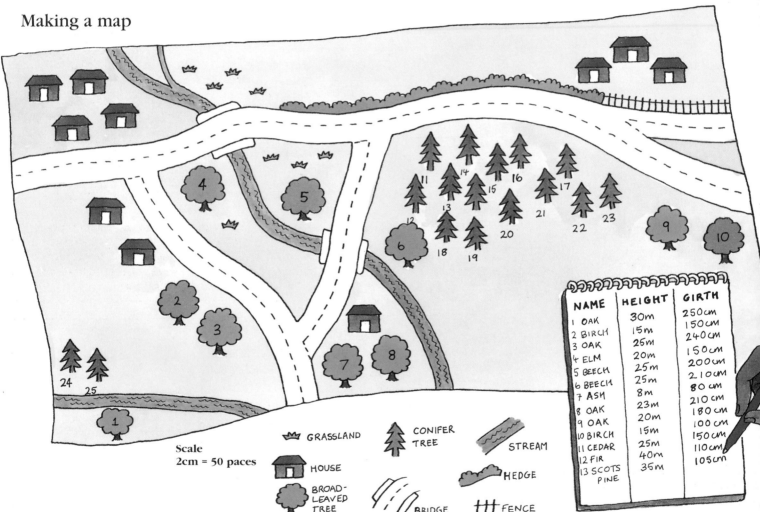

Scale
2cm = 50 paces

NAME	HEIGHT	GIRTH
1 OAK	30m	250cm
2 BIRCH	15m	150cm
3 OAK	25m	240cm
4 ELM	20m	150cm
5 BEECH	25m	200cm
6 BEECH	25m	210cm
7 ASH	8m	80cm
8 OAK	23m	210cm
9 OAK	20m	180cm
10 BIRCH	15m	100cm
11 CEDAR	25m	150cm
12 FIR	40m	110cm
13 SCOTS PINE	35m	105cm

Key:
- GRASSLAND
- HOUSE
- BROAD-LEAVED TREE
- CONIFER TREE
- BRIDGE
- STREAM
- HEDGE
- FENCE

After you have identified and measured the trees (as shown on these pages), make a neater and more detailed copy of your map. Show the scale of your map. Then make a key of the symbols you used, like the one above.

Write down the findings of your survey. Give the name, height and girth of each tree. Repeat the survey later to see if there are any new trees, or if anything else has changed. If you enjoyed making the survey, you can write to the Tree Council (see page 3 to find out how to do a more complicated one.

Measuring a tree

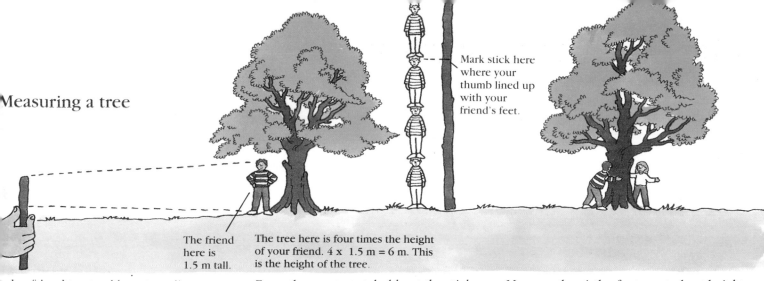

Mark stick here where your thumb lined up with your friend's feet.

The friend here is 1.5 m tall.

The tree here is four times the height of your friend. 4 x 1.5 m = 6 m. This is the height of the tree.

Ask a friend to stand by a tree. From a short distance, hold up a stick at arm's length. Line up the stick's tip with the top of your friend's head. Then move your thumb up the stick until it lines up with your friend's feet. Mark the tick where your thumb is.

From the same spot, hold out the stick again. How many times does the piece of stick above the mark go into the height of the tree. (Look carefully at the pictures here to see how this is done.) Now multiply the answer by your friend's height (1.5 m here).

Measure the girth of a tree at chest height. Ask your friend to hold one end of some string while you hold the other. Walk right around the tree until you meet your friend. Now measure the length of string.

Studying a tree

Squirrel's drey

Insects on the bark.

Nest

Do not touch birds' nests or go too near to them.

White sheet to catch insects.

Study the animals that live in or near your tree. Look for birds' nests and squirrels' dreys in the tree top. Look on the trunk for insects and on the ground for other traces of animals, such as owl pellets, and nuts or cones which have been eaten by animals. To examine the insects in the tree, beat a branch gently with a stick. With a white sheet, catch the insects that fall out.

Make a careful study of one tree all through the year. Choose a tree which you can get to easily and often. Make a notebook in which you keep a record of when it comes into leaf, when it flowers and fruits, and when it drops its leaves. Include sketches or photos of the tree at these different times and keep specimens from it.

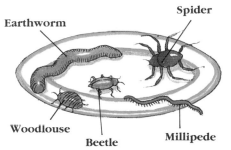

Leaf litter

Light bulb

Jar covered with black paper.

Funnel

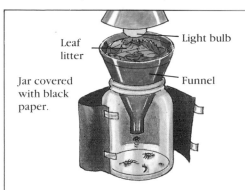

Earthworm

Spider

Woodlouse

Beetle

Millipede

Leaf litter is made up of dead and rotting leaves and contains many small animals. To study these animals, take a large funnel (or make one out of tin foil), and place it in a jar. Cover the jar with black paper. Fill the funnel with damp leaf litter. Place a lamp about 10 cm above the leaves and switch it on. Wait a few hours. The heat and light from the lamp will drive the animals into the dark jar. Then you can take them out and study them.

Common trees you can spot

Conifers

Lawson Cypress 25 m. Narrow shape. Drooping top shoot. Small, round cones. Common as a hedge.

Western Red Cedar 30 m. Branches curve upwards. Tiny, flower-like cones. Hedges.

Yew 15 m. Dark green. Trunk gnarled. Bark reddish. Leaves and red-berried fruits poisonous.

Western Hemlock 35 m. Branches and top shoot droop. Small cones. Needles various lengths.

Norway Spruce 30 m. Christmas tree. Long, hanging cones. Parks, gardens, plantations.

Douglas Fir 40 m. Hanging, shaggy cones. Deep-ridged bark. Important timber tree.

European Silver Fir 40 m. Large, upright cones at top of tree. Parklands.

Scots Pine 35 m. Uneven crown. Bare trunk. Flaking bark. Common wild and planted.

Corsican Pine 36 m. Shape rounder and fuller than Scots Pine. Long, dark green needles. Dark brown bark.

Blue Atlas Cedar 25 m. Broad shape. Barrel-shaped, upright cones. Blue-green needles. Parks.

European Larch 38 m. Upright cones egg-shaped. Soft, light-green needles fall off in winter.

Japanese Larch 35 m. Upright, rosette-like cones. Orange twigs. Blue-green needles fall in winter.

28

roadleaved trees

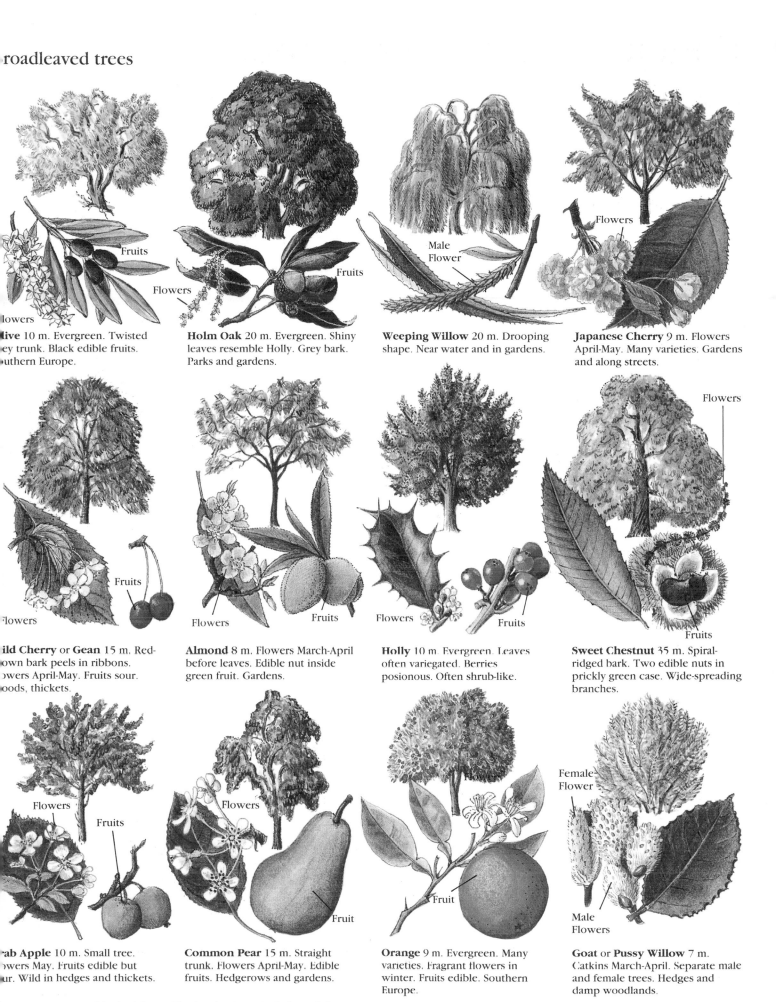

live 10 m. Evergreen. Twisted ey trunk. Black edible fruits. uthern Europe.

Holm Oak 20 m. Evergreen. Shiny leaves resemble Holly. Grey bark. Parks and gardens.

Weeping Willow 20 m. Drooping shape. Near water and in gardens.

Japanese Cherry 9 m. Flowers April-May. Many varieties. Gardens and along streets.

ild Cherry or **Gean** 15 m. Red-own bark peels in ribbons. wers April-May. Fruits sour. oods, thickets.

Almond 8 m. Flowers March-April before leaves. Edible nut inside green fruit. Gardens.

Holly 10 m. Evergreen. Leaves often variegated. Berries posionous. Often shrub-like.

Sweet Chestnut 35 m. Spiral-ridged bark. Two edible nuts in prickly green case. Wide-spreading branches.

ab Apple 10 m. Small tree. wers May. Fruits edible but ur. Wild in hedges and thickets.

Common Pear 15 m. Straight trunk. Flowers April-May. Edible fruits. Hedgerows and gardens.

Orange 9 m. Evergreen. Many varieties. Fragrant flowers in winter. Fruits edible. Southern Europe.

Goat or **Pussy Willow** 7 m. Catkins March-April. Separate male and female trees. Hedges and damp woodlands.

e trees are arranged by leaf shape. The height given is of a large full-grown tree.

29

More broadleaved trees

Common Beech 25 m. Smooth, grey bark. Nuts eaten by animals. Leaves can also be purple coloured.

Hornbeam 10 m. Smooth, grey, fluted trunk. Green winged fruits hanging in clusters. Hedges.

Wych Elm 20 m. Round, even crown. Woods and hedgerows. More common than English Elm in the north.

English Elm 30 m. Tall narrow crown, often irregular shape. Hedgerows and woods. Attacked by Dutch Elm Disease.

Whitebeam 8 m. Leaves white-felted underneath. Flowers May-June. Sour red berries. Grows wild.

Black Poplar 25 m. Dark trunk often with bumps. Common in city parks.

Silver Birch 15 m. White bark peels in ribbons. "Lamb's tail" catkins in April. Wild on heaths and mountains. Planted in gardens.

Common Alder 12 m. Cone-like fruits which stay on in winter. Catkins in early spring. Near water and damp woodlands.

Common Lime 25 m. Heart-shaped leaves. Fragrant flowers attract bees in June. Parks and gardens.

Turkey Oak 25 m. Whiskers on buds and at base of leaves. Acorn cups mossy. Bark ridged.

English or **Pedunculate Oak** 23 m. Wide-spreading branches. Long-stalked acorns. Common alone and in woods.

White Poplar 20 m. Leaves covered with white down underneath. Bark whitish-grey with diamond marks.

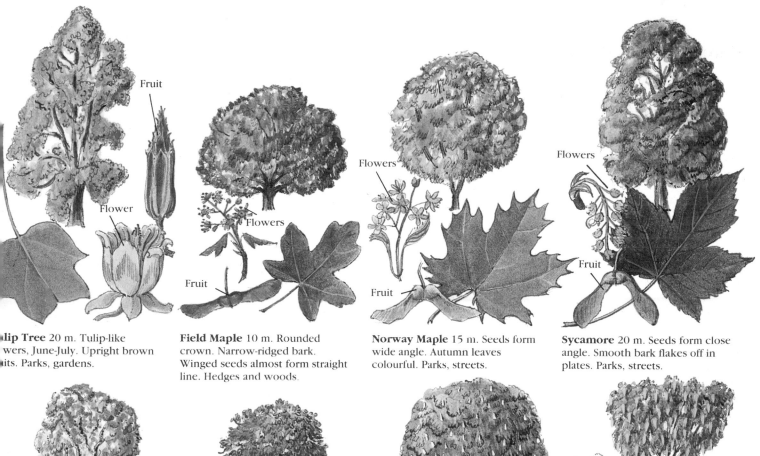

lip Tree 20 m. Tulip-like
wers, June-July. Upright brown
its. Parks, gardens.

Field Maple 10 m. Rounded
crown. Narrow-ridged bark.
Winged seeds almost form straight
line. Hedges and woods.

Norway Maple 15 m. Seeds form
wide angle. Autumn leaves
colourful. Parks, streets.

Sycamore 20 m. Seeds form close
angle. Smooth bark flakes off in
plates. Parks, streets.

ndon Plane 30 m. Bark flakes
leaving white patches. Spiky
its stay on in winter. City streets.

Fig 6 m. Flower inside a pear-
shaped receptacle which becomes
the fruit. Gardens.

Horse Chestnut 25 m. Compound
leaves. Upright flowers, May.
Prickly fruits with conkers inside.

Laburnum or **Golden Rain** 7 m.
Compound leaves. Flowers May-
June. Seeds poisonous. Gardens.

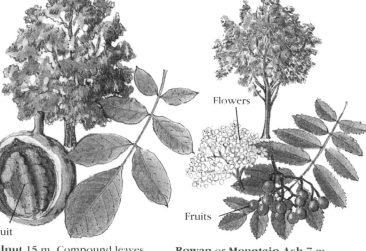

se Acacia or **Locust Tree** 20 m.
mpound leaves. Ridged twigs
ny. Hanging flowers, in June.
dens, parks.

Walnut 15 m. Compound leaves.
Deep-ridged bark. Hollow twigs.
Edible nuts inside thick green
fruits.

Rowan or **Mountain Ash** 7 m.
Compound leaves. Flowers May.
Sour orange berries, September.
Wild on mountains.

Common Ash 25 m. Compound
leaves open late. Key-shaped fruits
stay on in winter. Common
woods, parks.

Index

Acacia, False, 11, 17, 31
acorn, 16, 17, 18
Alder, Common, 11, 30
Almond, 29
Anemone, Wood, 25
annual rings, 20
Ant, wood, 24
Aphid, 22
Apple, 4, 18
    Crab, 15, 17, 29
Ash,
    Common, 8, 11, 17, 31
    Mountain, see Rowan
Badger, 25
bark, 5, 6, 13, 20, 21, 22, 23
    rubbings, 13
Bat, Long-eared, 25
Beech,
    Common, 6, 7, 9, 11, 13, 30
    Copper, 8, 9
bees, 4
Beetle, 27
    Cockchafer, 22
    Elm Bark, 22
    Greater Stag, 25
Birch, Silver, 9, 10, 13, 12, 30
Bluebell, 25
Box, 6
Bracken, 24
broadleaved trees, 5, 6, 8, 12, 16, 17, 19,
    21, 24, 25, 29-31
buds, 4, 5, 7, 10-11
    leader, 4
Butterfly, Speckled Wood, 25
cambium, 5, 20
carbon dioxide, 24
caterpillar, Tent, 22
catkins, 11, 15
Cedar,
    Blue Atlas, 8, 28
    of Lebanon, 16
    Western Red, 28
Cherry, 17
    Japanese, 14, 29
    Wild, 11, 29
Chestnut,
    Horse, 4, 7, 8, 9, 10, 31
    Sweet, 11, 17, 18, 29
chipboard, 21
chlorophyll, 5, 8, 9
cones, 16
Conifer Heart Rot, 22
conifer trees, 5, 7, 8, 16, 19, 21, 24, 28
conker, 7
coppicing, 12
cork, 13

Crossbill, 24
Cypress, Lawson, 8, 28
Deer, 23
    Red, 24
    Roe, 25
Earthworm, 25, 27
Elm,
    English, 11, 12, 17, 30
    Wych, 30
Fern, Broad Buckler, 24
fertilization, 15
Fig, 7, 31
Fir,
    Douglas, 16, 19, 28
    European Silver, 16, 28
fire tower, 19
flowers, 4, 7, 14
    perfect, 14,
Fly Agaric, 24
forestry, 19
Forsythia, 10
Fox, 24
fruits, 4, 7, 14, 16-17
fungus, 22-23
    Honey, 22
galls, 22, 23
    Oak Apple, 22, 23
Gean, 29
girdle scar, 4, 5, 20
Goldcrest, 24
Golden Rain, 31
grain, 21
greenhouse effect, 24
Green Tortrix, 22
Grouse, Black, 24
hardwood, 6, 21
Hazel, 7
heartwood, 5, 20
Hedgehog, 25
Holly, 5, 8, 29
Hornbeam, 30
humus, 24
insects, 6, 15, 22
Ivy, 25
Juniper, 16
knots, 21
Laburnum, 31
Larch,
    European, 7, 14, 16, 28
    Japanese, 28
Laurel, 6
leaves, 4, 5, 6, 8-9, 22
    litter, 27
lichen, 24
Lime, Common 6, 8, 11, 12, 30
Locust Tree, 31

Looper, Pine, 22
Magnolia, 11
Maidenhair Tree, 9
Maple,
    Field, 8, 31
    Japanese, 6
    Norway, 6, 31
Millipede, 27
Miner, Leaf, 22
Mistletoe, 25
moss, 25
nectar, 4
Nuthatch, 25
nuts, 17
Oak, 7, 19, 22, 23, 25
    Cork, 13
    English or Pedunculate, 6, 8, 12,
    13, 30
    Holm, 6, 29
    Red, 9
    Turkey, 11, 30
Olive, 29
Orange, 18 ,29
ovary, 14, 15, 17
ovule, 14, 15, 16, 17
Owl,
    Long-eared, 24
    Tawny, 25
oxygen, 7
palm trees, 7, 20
Palm, Canary, 7
Peach, 17
Pear, Common, 9, 29
pests, 22-23
Pheasant, 25
phloem, 5, 13, 20
Pine,
    Corsican, 8, 28
    Scots, 5, 7, 12, 13, 16, 28
    Stone, 16
Pine Marten, 24
Plane, London, 6, 11, 17, 31
plantation, 19
plywood, 21
pollarding, 12
pollen, 4, 14, 15
pollination, 14, 15
Poor Man's Beefsteak, 25
Poplar,
    Black, 8, 30
    Lombardy, 6, 12
    White, 9, 11, 30
Primrose, 25
Rabbit, 23, 25
ray, 5, 20
Redwood, Dawn, 9

Roller, Leaf, 22
Rook, 25,
roots, 22
Rowan, 9, 17, 31
sap, 5, 13, 20
sapwood, 5, 20
Sawfly, Pine, 22
Scale, 22
seasoning, 21
seeds, 4, 7, 14, 16-17, 18, 19
seedling, 4, 5, 18, 19
sepal, 14
shape, 6, 12
shoots, 22
Shrew, Common, 25
Slug, Black, 24
softwood, 6, 21
spider, 27
spore, 22, 23
    prints, 23
Spruce, Norway, 7, 8, 10, 12, 16, 28
Squirel, 23
    drey, 24
    Red, 24
stamen, 14
stigma, 14, 15
style, 15
Sycamore, 4, 6, 7, 11, 18, 31
Timberman, 24
Tit, Blue, 25
Toad, Common, 25
Treecreeper, 24
tree survey, 26-27
Tulip Tree, 7, 31
twigs, 9, 10-11, 20
veneer, 21
Vole, Field, 23
Walnut, 11, 17, 31
Wasp, Gall, 22
Weevil,
    Nut, 22
    Pine, 22
Western Hemlock, 16, 28
White Pine Blister Rust, 22
Whitebeam, 11, 30
Willow, 10, 11, 14, 17
    Crack, 8, 15
    Pussy or Goat, 29
    Weeping, 6, 12, 29
wood, 21, 22
    pulp, 21
Woodlouse, 27
Woodpecker,
    Great Spotted, 24
    Green, 25
Yew, 6, 14, 16, 28

Books

Trees. (Collins Green Guides)
Trees of Britain and Europe. Bob
    Gibbons (W.H. Smiths' Field
    Naturalist's Library)
Trees of Britain and Europe. Bob Press
    (Green Guide - New Holland)
Conifers. The Forestry Commision
    (H.M.S.O.)
The Observer's Bok of Trees.
    W.J.Stokoe (Warne)

Clubs and national organizations

The Council for Environmental Conservation (80 York Way, London, N1 9AG) will supply the addresses of your local **Natural History Societies**. Send an s.a.e. for the list.

The Royal Society for the Protection of Nature (Vigilant House, 120 Wilton Road, London SW1V 1J2) will give you the address of your local **County Naturalist Trust**, which may have a junior branch. Many of the Trusts have meetings and lectures, and offer opportunities for work on nature reserves.

The Tree Council (35 Belgrave Square, London, SW1 8QB) produces many leaflets and booklets, including one called Making a Tree Survey.

The Council for the Protection of Rural England (Warwick House, 25 Buckingham Palace Road, London SW1W 0PP) has many leaflets and posters. Leaflets can also be obtained from **The Forestry Commission**, Information Branch, 235 Corstorphine Road, Edinburgh EH12 7AT.

The Botanical Society of the British Isles, c/o Natural History Museum, Cromwell Road, London, SW7 5BD

English Nature, Northminster House, Peterborough OE1 1UA

The Countryside Commission, John Dower House, Crescent Place, Cheltenham, Gloucestershire GL50 3RA